I0068199

Shopify Dropshipping: How to Make Money From Home, Make Passive Online Income, and Achieve Financial Freedom Through Your Own Online Ecommerce Business

by Ben Gothard,

Founder & CEO of Gothard Enterprises LLC

Author of CEO at 20: A Little Book for Big Dreams

Text and Illustration Copyright © 2017 by Benjamin
Pressner Gothard. All rights reserved.

All rights reserved. This book or parts thereof may not be
reproduced in any form, stored in any retrieval system, or
transmitted in any form by any means — electronic,
mechanical, photocopy, recording, or otherwise — without
prior written permission of the publisher, except as
provided by United States of America copyright law. For
permission requests, contact the publisher at:

bgothard@gothardenterprises.com

ISBN: 0997812486

ISBN-13: 978-0997812480

Shopify Dropshipping

Do you dream of being financially free? To be able to take vacations around the world at your leisure and have the ability to make money with nothing more than a laptop or a smart phone is liberating. How about extra income? Would an extra $500 per month make an impact on your life? What about an extra $5,000 per month? $50,000? Owning your own business is your ticket to becoming not only financially secure, but *wealthy*. Anybody can do it, including you! However, you will give yourself the best chance of success by find the right business model for you (among other things).

In this book, I am going to talk to you about Shopify Dropshipping. I recently come across this phenomenon and it is probably one of the easiest ways that I've ever found to get started making passive income and build a sustainable online business. In this book, I'm going give you an overview of the platform and show you step-by-step of exactly how to do it. By reading on, you will be exposed to a business model that allows the owner to work from anywhere, at anytime, with a phone or a laptop and an Internet connection. I don't work for Shopify, nor am I invested in the company in any way. I wrote this book because I have made and will continue to make money on the Shopify platform, and I think that ANYBODY can leverage this business model to build passive income and become financially free. I am passionate about helping entrepreneurs build their skills and develop assets that will allow them to chase their dreams.

Before we dive into the technicality of this process, however, I want to preface my system by saying that while this IS one of the easiest ways to get started making passive income and has one of the lowest start-up costs and barriers to entry of any business I have come across, this IS NOT going to happen by itself. You need to put in the work. By using this system you are starting a business, and starting a business will ALWAYS be a difficult process. Getting traction with a new concept/product/service will NEVER be a walk in the park. I don't say this to scare you away. Rather, I want to make sure that you know what you are getting yourself into. There is no such thing as a "get rich quick" scheme. There will never be a magical button you press that will instantly put millions of dollars into your bank account. It is up to you to build your business up and become successful.

Starting a business is a commitment. It is a commitment to yourself and your customers to follow through with what you said you were going to do and deliver what you said you were going to deliver. Nobody is going to hold your hand through this process, and, at first, chances are you are going to fail. A lot. If you aren't okay with that, then you might want to stop now and go get a job. However, if you are ready to start your entrepreneurial journey and reach financial independence, read on. You won't be sorry!

The Process

At a bird's eye view, dropshipping on Shopify means selling a product that gets shipped directly from your supplier to the customer. You start by picking a product to sell and finding a reliable supplier. I recommend using AliExpress, or some sort of website that allows you to find suppliers who offer wholesale prices and will sell individual units. Then you mark it up for retail, and sell that product to the customer for profit (the difference between what it costs you to buy the product and the markup you are able to sell the product with). But here's the beauty of the system: the customer buys it from you **before** you buy it from the supplier. Just to be clear, the customer buys it from you, and **then** you buy it from your supplier. As if that wasn't convenient enough for you, the supplier sends it straight to the customer on your behalf. You don't have to worry about manufacturing, inventory, storage, packaging, labeling or shipping. Just to be clear, the customer buys the product from you, you buy the product from your supplier and the supplier sends it right to the customer. You don't have to touch the product!

Sound too good to be true? This ecommerce business model is a fantastic way to begin your entrepreneurship journey, because it takes a lot of the cost and time requirements out of the retail business. Having to design a product, get it patented, manufactured, stored, and delivered to the customer adds an enormous amount of hassle and expense to your business. Not to mention, in order to get something manufactured (in most factories), you need to invest a significant amount of capital upfront in inventory. For example, a lot of factories overseas require a $10,000 initial investment to even turn on the machine and start manufacturing your product.

Now, I'm not saying that this business model is perfect, and I will cover some weak points later in this book. However, for a new entrepreneur, dropshipping on Shopify is one of the fastest, easiest and most cost effective ways to get started making passive income and building a real business. That being said, I don't want to spend any more time talking about WHY you should invest your time and effort into this business. Instead, lets dive into exactly HOW you can get your own Shopify dropshipping business up and running in less than a day.

The beauty of a Shopify store is that you can set one up in less than an hour once you're familiar with the process. Here is the Shopify website:

An ecommerce platform made for you

Whether you sell online, on social media, in store, or out of the trunk of your car, Shopify has you covered.

| Enter your email address | Get started |

All you have to do in order to get started on this process is to put in your e-mail address. Then, they're going to ask you to create a password and store name. One word of caution - when you are deciding on a store name, it's good to think about it a little bit before you jump right in. Although you can change your store name, there are two reasons why I would recommend doing some research before immediately getting into your site. First, the default URL is set when you first enter your store name into the box and it will take some extra dollars to fix it. Second, and most importantly, it is critical for you to understand what kind of store you want to set up before you get started. Determining what you want to sell will influence the name, aesthetic design (does it look nice?), and functional design (can people quickly and easily find what they want?) of your store. Unless you are innovative and come up with a unique approach, I'd recommend using one of two major store types.

The first type is a store that sells a lot of things, and you don't really have that big of a focus on any one type of product in particular. This store model is more of general store like Walmart or Target. Instead of competing on specific, high quality products, this type of store generally competes on price, a wide selection of products, and plenty of inventory. The second type is a niche store where you pick one specific industry (sports & outdoors), or one specific niche within an industry (fishing supplies), and you sell items that are directly related to that niche.

What you want to sell really depends on you, but I recommend sticking to what you know. When you stick to products that you are already familiar with, you will have a much greater ability to judge product quality without any further research. For example, let's say that you want to sell high-quality fishing line to fishing guides. If you are an expert on fishing supplies already, then you will know good line from poor. You'll know that different pound tackle is needed for the various fishing conditions that your market will face. You won't make as many mistakes selling the wrong type of line for the wrong purpose. A customer who wants to go fly-fishing in a fast moving creek in North Carolina will have completely different needs than a customer who is trawling for massive tuna in the Gulf of Mexico. As a fisherman or woman yourself, you will already be familiar with the ins-and-outs of the industry. By already having that experience, you will be able to cut down significantly on your learning curve of building your own business. If you know which niche you want to sell in, it would probably be more advantageous for you to start out in that niche immediately.

However, if you don't already know what you want to sell or are looking to start fresh, I would recommend a general store because you have flexibility to test different products in whichever industries you want. Once you find products that are successful, then you might consider taking those same products and putting them into a niche store to build off of the initial success. This method will allow you to focus in on what works and build a store off of products that are already selling for you! Keep testing out new products in your general store, and then move those products into niche stores once you figure out what works.

After entering in your personal information in the second window that you see, you are going come across the third page like below:

Tell us a little about yourself

ARE YOU ALREADY SELLING?

Please choose one...

HOW MUCH REVENUE DOES YOUR BUSINESS CURRENTLY MAKE IN A YEAR?

Please choose one...

ARE YOU SETTING UP A STORE FOR A CLIENT?

Yes, I'm designing/developing a store for a client

‹ Back   Enter my store

This is simply Shopify's way of collecting a little bit of data. They want to know if you're already selling and your current annual revenue. Based on your answers, they're going to offer you customized pieces of advice. Your answers to these questions have no impact on your store. Pick what is most applicable to you. Once you are ready, enter your store!

The first thing that I would recommend you do is install a few useful Shopify applications that will help you to succeed. Typically, you would go over to the application section and click "Visit Shopify App Store" as seen below:

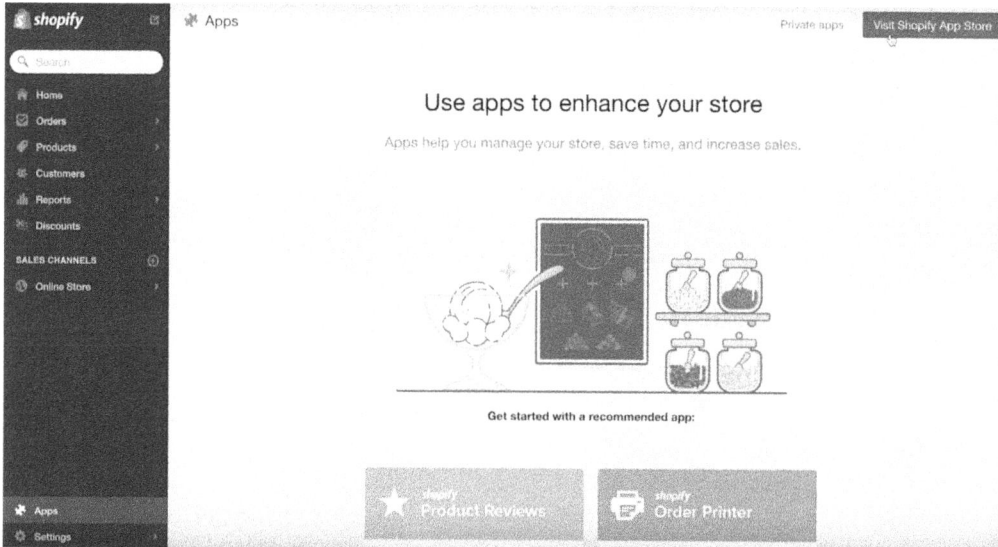

Whereas most people look through tons and tons of apps and try to figure out the best ones, I wanted to give you a little bonus gift by not only picking out the three apps that I *always* use in every store that I have created. I've taken the time to test many different variations of apps that performed similar functions, and through experimentation these three apps are my favorite. The first one is Chilliapp's Abandonment Protector. This app is very useful for retargeting using e-mail marketing campaigns. When somebody goes to your store and puts an item in their cart and proceeds to checkout but then they don't checkout, Abandonment Protector will automate the e-mail recapturing process. You can set up these e-mail templates that will be sent out to customers with different coupon codes or just an e-mail reminding them to come back--anything that you can do to get in front of the customer again.

The second app is Beeketing's Boost Sales – whenever somebody adds something to cart, this app will automatically upsell or cross sell them based on the settings you set. I prefer upsells but you can do either one. With this app, you can turn a sale that would've been $3.99 into a sale that makes you $59.99, $159.99, etc. Tools like this are very useful for you to maximizing your single customer revenue. Earnings per customer can be driven upwards by utilizing Beeketing's Boost Sales. As a general rule, I would always try to upsell *related* items to your customers. For example, let's say that you sell 100ft of fishing line for $10. When the consumer adds that item to their cart, why not suggest a 500ft bundle of the same fishing line for $40! Not only does the customer get a better deal on what he or she already wanted, but you get to move more units at once.

The third one is going to make your life so so so much easier! With this app, you can basically automate the whole process of dropshipping. It's called Oberlo, and it allows you to go into AliExpress (one of the cheapest places to find your products) and import products directly into your store. Instead of having to manually add products and filling out tons of different information, Oberlo gives you the option to import products and the accompanying information with just one click of a button.

At this stage you need to pick a theme for your story. The theme is important because it sets the tone for your customers. The aesthetics and utility of your store are a crucial part to making or breaking the consumer experience. Taking time to think through how you want to engage your website visitors and deliberately pick a theme that will help you accomplish your goal. While you can buy some themes by visiting the "Theme Store," there are plenty of quality free themes that you can pick from as seen below:

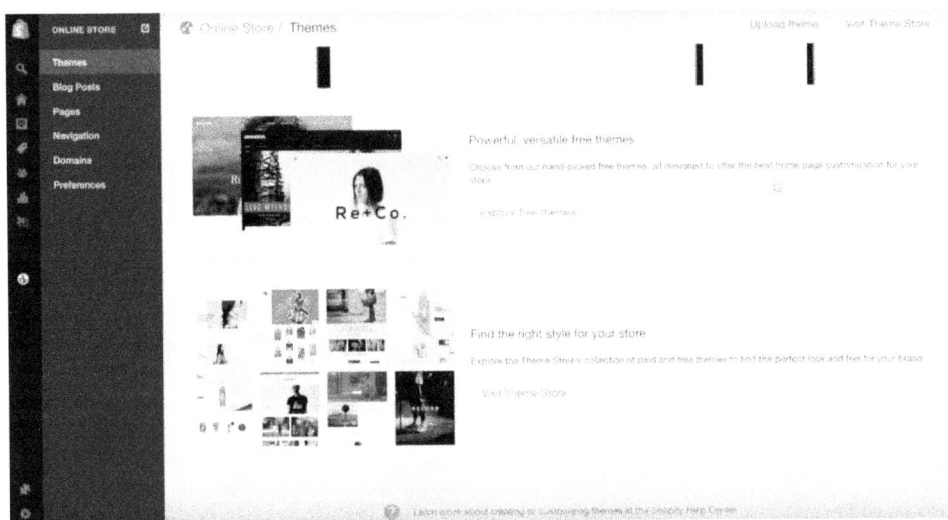

If you are a total beginner, I would recommend picking something really simple and product focused. Your theme is not the most crucial piece of this process, and don't fret if you don't like the first theme that you pick. You can easily change at anytime, or customize the theme that you already have. By the way! For those of you who are hesitant to start a store because you don't think that you can build a website and/or you don't know how to code, this is the easiest way I have found to make a decent website. Now you have no more excuses, and there is no better time to start your own dropshipping business today.

Next, you are going to customize your theme! I'd suggest starting off by tackling the homepage first, as seen below:

While it may seem a daunting task to find a nice big image for your homepage, fear not! There are plenty of opportunities that you can take advantage of if you are creative, but I want to present you with two major options.

Option 1: Let's say that you need to find a high-quality picture for your camping store. Simply go search "camping" on Google Images and change the usage rights to "labeled for reuse" as seen below:

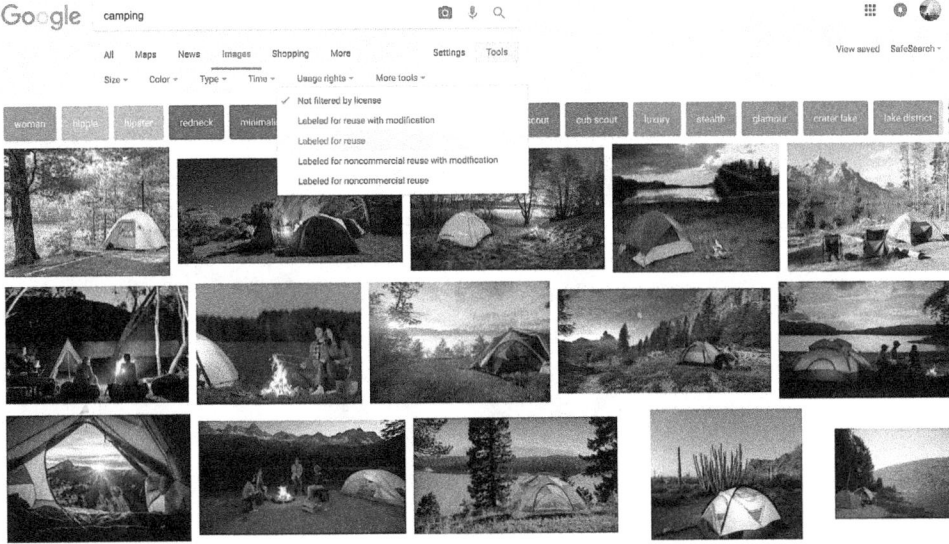

Option 2: Alternatively, you can go to <u>Canva</u> and create your own design based off of high-quality stock templates provided by <u>Canva</u>. You can actually use this tool for any of your graphic design needs. When you login to the website, you can create a new design and pick from **a ton** of options (not all shown) as seen below:

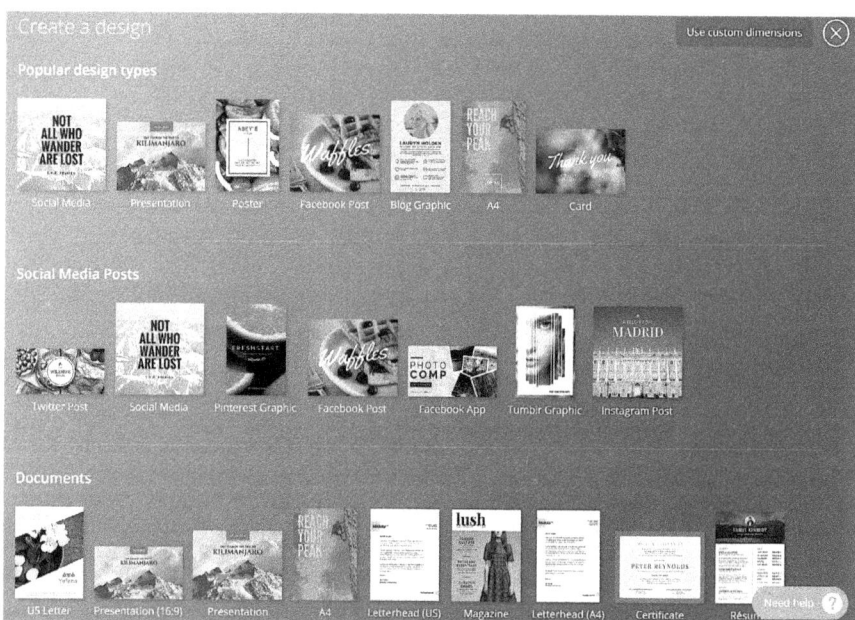

You just pick your design, and if you do one of their template designs, Canva will actually give you high-quality examples that you can tweak to fit your needs.

Both of these options take a lot of the pressure off the graphic design side of the business. You don't have to design and create extravagant images from scratch to build a website that converts. As long as your site is aesthetically pleasing and easy to navigate, you can start. A lot of people get hung up on trying to be **perfect** from day one. The truth is, when you are first building your business, you're not going to be the best. That is okay! There are people who have been doing this successfully for years. It's going to take time to learn the business, but you have the advantage with this particular type of business – it is **easy** to start and the upside of being successful is complete financial freedom.

Now that you have your store, you need some products! Full disclosure, I'm not going to go **too** in-depth into the product selection process in this book. I want to give you the tools to pick products now. Whenever you are going about finding things to sell in your store, I would highly recommend that you do research beyond the scope of this particular book. For teaching purposes, let's start the process by going to AliExpress. Again, there are different strategies for finding products but for the sake of this video I'm just going to go to the best-selling, as seen below:

Let's say that you wanted to sell the second product, fleece beanies.

Because we downloaded Oberlo (there is a chrome extension), all you have to do is press the little blue button in the bottom right of the photo below

and the product is immediately imported into your store:

See the little green checkmark in the top right of the picture above?

That means that your item has been successfully imported into your store.

Now you can go back to your store, click on the apps button, click on

Oberlo, and open your import list as seen below:

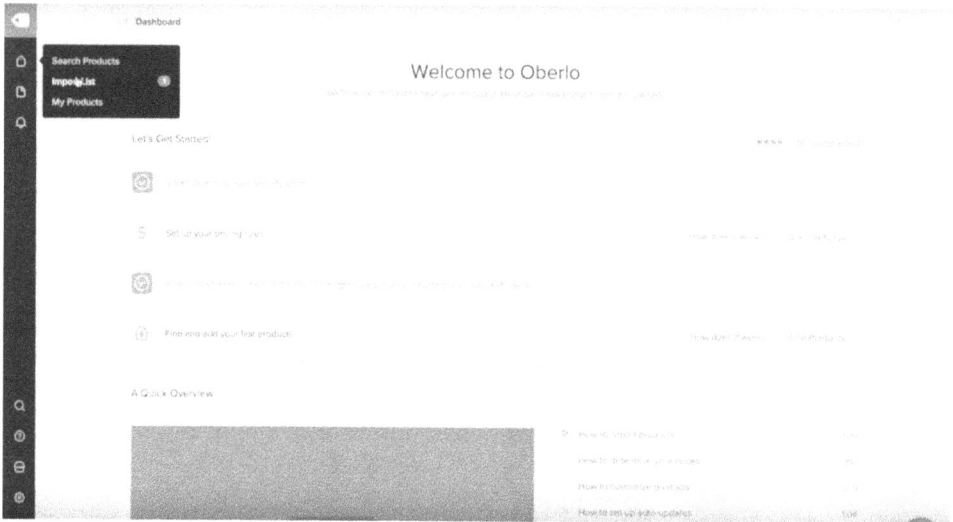

Oberlo took all of the data from here—from this AliExpress page and is now importing this into your store – and it gets even better. If you want to edit any of the information that the app pulled from AliExpress, you can easily do so at this step. The name of your product is important, but I'll piece of the puzzle up to you. Collection and Type are next, and these identifiers are how you can organize your products for your customers. Make sure it is intuitive and easy to navigate! Tags are next, and these are primarily for SEO optimization. I'm not an expert on Shopify SEO optimization, so I won't be going into that in this book. Let's move on to the description, as seen below:

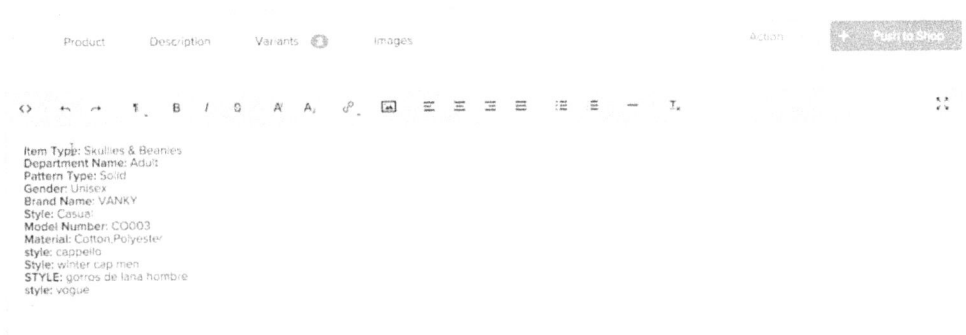

As a general rule, if what is imported isn't necessary, get rid of it. I'd suggest keeping the brand name in (unless you are private labeling), you more than likely didn't create the product – you're just selling it. The biggest opportunity in this section is the opportunity to write up a compelling product description. I'd do some research on copywriting and get creative with your own product description. This is a way for you to stand out from your competition and establish a brand voice.

	Product	Description	Variants	Images					Action	Push to Shop

	Use all	SKU	Color		Cost	Price		Compared At Price	Inventory
						Change your price		Change your price	
☑		943901-black	Black		$3.59	3.59		3.59	460
☑		943901-dark-grey	Dark Grey		$3.43	3.43		3.43	485
☑		943901-blue	Blue		$2.99	2.99		2.99	499

Next are your variants (seen above) and this is a cool feature because Oberlo recognizes that one product may have more than color or size with different price points for each one. By having different variants available, you have the ability to reach more people with one product. Some people might really like this hat in black, some people might really like this face mask in dark grey. The variants you include in your store should depend on what your customers want. You want to keep the prices consistent and fair, but you are also trying to make money off this. At full cost, each unit is roughly $8.60, so you need to put your price over $8.60. Also, keep in mind that you have to take into marketing costs, shipping costs, administrative costs (Shopify + the apps). In other words, you have to cover all your expenses and then have enough left over to make it worth your time. In my experience, I would say that you can probably sell this item to the right niche, in the right market, for $15.99 maybe $16.99. When you are picking your own products to sell, make sure that you can cover all of your margins and bring in enough profit to make it worth your while.

The next step is to pick your images, and choosing high-quality photos is critical. A lot of credibility can be built or lost with your customers based on these images. As a general rule, I would only include images that show the exact product. For example, don't make people think they are getting an entire cutlery set when you are selling a single knife. Make sure to include different perspectives of the product. You want to give your customers as much information as possible because that will give your prospective buyers confidence in your store. Choose pictures on your product page very deliberately, you never know how somebody is going to interpret your photo. Once you do that, you simply push this item to your shop and your Shopify store will be automatically updated to include the product.

Now that you have a product, you face another decision. Do you want to focus on one single product, a few select products, or an entire store with a full catalog? There is no right or wrong answer here, and there are examples of successful stores for each option. If you are happy with one product, great! You are ready for the next step. If you'd like to specialize in a few products, you have some more research to do and items to add to your store before you are ready for the next step. If you want an entire store with a full catalog, you have a lot more work ahead of you before you are ready for the next step. One suggestion for the third option is to make sure that all of your items are high quality. Just because you have quantity doesn't mean you have quality, and it is quality that will help you build a long-term sustainable business.

With your product(s) ready to go, it's time to start sending traffic to your store. You need a marketing strategy. That being said, everybody's marketing strategy is a little bit different, and nobody does the exact same thing or markets the same way. You are going to need to develop your own strategy over time, and different industries will have their own nuances that you must account for. The fastest way I've come across to get website visitors is to use Facebook to send very highly targeted traffic directly to the Shopify product page. For example, I would send traffic to the product imported above that consisted of people who liked skiing or who live in cold places and need a facemask like this. The beauty of using Facebook is that you can target people based on their interest and target the people who are most likely to buy your product. I would target brands that sell products similar to your own and have large followings on Facebook. Sending people straight from Facebook to your product page provides the least amount of friction possible. In other words, the customer has very little clicking to do before the buy button on your site.

Now you see the power of Shopify dropshipping! In less than an hour, you can start your own business with an e-mail address. If somebody goes to your store and clicks add to cart and pays, that money goes to you. The customer is legitimately going to get a bill from your store. The best part is that once you get a purchase order, you can see and fulfill orders through Oberlo. It will take you back to AliExpress and add the correct item to your cart with accurate shipping information provided by the customer automatically. You don't have to worry about mistyping anything or not knowing what to do, the app guides you through it all.

Shopify is a great opportunity to make passive income, and know you have a better grasp of how easy it is. Just to reiterate, whenever you get an order, the customer buys it from you, and then you buy it from your supplier. Starting a business like this costs you nothing but your time. The only cost to you is marketing, and as you build your skills in that regard that expense will drop significantly. The only thing that you have to do is fill the orders once you make sales, and eventually you can hire an assistant to do that for you. The upfront time investment is product selection and marketing. Besides that, Shopify dropshipping is one of the fastest ways to build passive income that I've ever come across.

My final suggestion would be to enjoy the journey. Not every path will end up where you think it will, and what you learn about the world and yourself may be worth more to you than the original goal. Find passion for your journey, because you have a long and winding road ahead of you. There is greater strength within yourself than you know, and once you fully believe in your ability to accomplish incredible things, you will be amazed what you can do. Good luck on your business-building journey! Who knows? You might even have a little fun along the way.

www.ingramcontent.com/pod-product-compliance
Lightning Source LLC
Chambersburg PA
CBHW070922210326
41521CB00010B/2280

* 9 7 8 0 9 9 7 8 1 2 4 8 0 *